365 Days of Positivity: A Year of Inspiration

SAMY B

365 Days of Positivity: A Year of Inspiration

Table of Contents:

Chapter 1: Introduction - A Year of Positivity

- The concept of a year-long journey of positivity
- The significance of maintaining a positive mindset

Chapter 2: Positivity Unleashed

- The essence of positivity and its power
- Choosing a positive outlook to transform life

Chapter 3: Daily Doses of Love and Inspiration

- The idea of receiving daily doses of love and inspiration
- Love and inspiration as driving forces behind a positive life

Chapter 4: A Year of Success and Courage

- The role of success and courage in a positive life
- Daily quotes as motivation and determination

Chapter 5: Finding Your Joy

- Finding joy in everyday life
- The contribution of simple moments to overall positivity

Chapter 6: The Path to Positivity and Success

- Daily reminders leading to positivity and success
- Emphasizing small steps for personal growth

Chapter 7: A Year of Love, Hope, and Happiness

- Embracing love, hope, and happiness in daily life
- The enhancement of positivity through these emotions

Chapter 8: Unleash Your Potential

- Focusing on unlocking potential with daily quotes
- Realizing one's capabilities and dreams

Chapter 9: A Brighter Tomorrow

- The role of positivity in creating a brighter future
- Inspiring hope and motivating change through daily quotes

Chapter 10: A Life Well-Lived

- Reflecting on the journey undertaken throughout the year
- The impact of living a life well-lived on oneself and others

Conclusion: Carrying Positivity Forward

- Reiterating the importance of carrying positivity into life
- Encouraging readers to continue their journey of inspiration and share their positivity with the world

Quotes :

25 Quotes to Illuminate Your Day with Radiance

25 Heartwarming Love Quotes to Ignite the Soul

25 Inspirational Quotes for Unwavering Motivation

25 Uplifting Quotes to Elevate Your Spirit

25 Inspirational Quotes to Ignite Courage

25 Inspirational Quotes to Illuminate Your Path with Hope

100 Quotes for a Richer, Healthier, and Happier You

365 Days of Positivity: A Year of Inspiration

Chapter 1: Introduction - A Year of Positivity

As the sun dipped below the horizon, casting a warm orange glow across the evening sky, Emma sat down in her favorite cozy armchair. She clutched the book she had just received as a gift, "365 Days of Positivity: A Year of Inspiration," in her hands. The cover was adorned with a vibrant, uplifting design that seemed to beckon her into its pages.

With a sense of anticipation, Emma opened the book to Chapter 1. The title, "A Year of Positivity," was like a promise of something wonderful to come. She knew she was about to embark on a journey, a year-long journey of positivity through daily quotes, and she couldn't wait to see where it would lead.

The first chapter introduced Emma to the concept of the year-long journey she was about to undertake. It emphasized the importance of maintaining a positive mindset and the profound impact it could have on one's life. Emma had always been a firm believer in the power of positivity, and this book felt like the perfect companion for her journey.

As she read, she found herself nodding in agreement with the author's words. The book explained how a positive mindset could transform one's life, how it could be the key to unlocking new opportunities, and how it could make even the darkest days a little brighter. Emma felt a renewed sense of hope and determination.

She thought about her own life and the challenges she had faced over the years. There had been moments of doubt and despair, but she had always found a way to bounce back, to see the silver lining in every cloud. This book, she realized, would be a daily reminder to continue on that path of positivity.

As she finished the first chapter, Emma closed the book and took a deep breath. She knew that the year ahead would be filled with ups and downs, but with each daily quote, she would be inspired to keep moving forward. She felt a deep sense of gratitude for the gift of this book and the opportunity to start this incredible journey.

With a smile on her face, Emma placed the book on her bedside table, ready to open it again the next morning and discover what new nugget of wisdom and positivity awaited her. Little did she know that this book would become a constant companion, a source of inspiration, and a guiding light through the year ahead.

Chapter 2: Positivity Unleashed

With each passing day, Emma found herself diving deeper into the essence of positivity. The daily quotes had become her guiding stars, illuminating the path toward a brighter, more optimistic outlook on life. She had embraced the challenge of a year-long journey with unwavering determination.

As she flipped to the second chapter, "Positivity Unleashed," she was eager to explore the essence of positivity and its transformative power. Emma had always considered herself a realist, but now she understood that a positive outlook could be the key to unlocking the doors of endless possibilities.

The first quote in this chapter read, **"Positivity is the ember that ignites the fire of your spirit. It has the power to turn dreams into reality and obstacles into stepping stones."** The words resonated with Emma, reminding her that she held the power to shape her destiny.

With renewed enthusiasm, she took the quote to heart. She realized that a positive mindset was not just about wishful thinking; it was about choosing to see the silver lining in every situation. It was about embracing challenges as opportunities for growth.

As the days turned into weeks, Emma's perspective on life began to shift. She found herself seeking out the positive aspects of even the most challenging situations. Instead of dwelling on failures, she saw them as valuable lessons. And when obstacles arose, she approached them with resilience and unwavering determination.

Emma's friends and family noticed the change in her. They saw her as a source of inspiration, someone who could find the good even in the darkest of times. Emma had become a beacon of positivity, and it was all thanks to the daily quotes that had ignited her spirit.

Chapter 2 had set the tone for the rest of the year. Emma was no longer just a realist; she had become a fervent believer in the power of positivity. She knew that this journey was just beginning, and there was so much more to discover in the chapters that lay ahead.

As she closed the book for the day, Emma couldn't help but feel a sense of gratitude. She was grateful for the opportunity to embark on this journey, to explore the depths of positivity, and to witness the incredible transformation it was bringing to her life. Emma had unleashed the power of positivity, and there was no turning back.

Chapter 3: Daily Doses of Love and Inspiration

The sun pecked through the curtains, casting a warm glow over Emma's room as she sat at her favorite corner, a cozy nook where her collection of daily quotes had grown over the past months. With each day, she had delved deeper into the world of positivity, embracing its profound impact on her life.

Chapter 3, "Daily Doses of Love and Inspiration," had a special place in Emma's heart. It spoke to her soul, reminding her of the importance of love and inspiration in her journey toward a more positive and fulfilling life.

The first quote in this chapter read, **"Love and inspiration are the fuel for a heart that shines brightly. Let them be the driving forces behind your actions, and watch how they light up your world."** Emma marveled at how these words encapsulated the essence of her journey.

As she contemplated the quote, Emma realized that love and inspiration were the foundations of her newfound positivity. Love had the power to strengthen bonds, create joy, and bring solace in times of need. Inspiration was the spark that ignited her passions and fueled her determination to live her best life.

Emma looked around her room, at the photographs of loved ones and the books that had inspired her along the way. She thought of the friends who had encouraged her and the mentors who had guided her. It was in these connections and the experiences that had shaped her that she found the wellspring of love and inspiration.

With each passing day, Emma was determined to share this love and inspiration with the world. She reached out to friends and family, offering words of encouragement and acts of kindness. She began to mentor others, sharing her journey of positivity and inspiring them to embark on their own.

In this chapter, Emma discovered that love and inspiration were not finite resources; they multiplied when shared. As she sipped her morning tea, she made a promise to herself to be a beacon of love and inspiration for others, just as the daily quotes had been for her.

The days turned into weeks, and Emma's journey continued. She marveled at how love and inspiration had become her daily companions, guiding her steps and infusing her life with purpose and joy. This chapter had shown her that the more she gave, the more she received in return.

As she closed the book for the day, Emma couldn't help but smile. She had learned that love and inspiration were not distant ideals; they were tangible forces that could transform her life and the lives of those around her. With a heart full of love and a spirit brimming with inspiration, Emma was ready to face whatever the journey had in store.

Chapter 4: A Year of Success and Courage

Emma's journey through the year of positivity continued, and the next chapter beckoned with a promise of success and courage. As she opened the book to Chapter 4, she couldn't help but feel a sense of anticipation. The daily quotes had already instilled in her a newfound sense of purpose and optimism, and she was ready to explore the role of success and courage in her life.

The first quote in this chapter read, **"Success and courage are the inseparable companions of those who dare to dream and persist. They are the armor that shields you from doubt and the wings that carry you to new heights."** Emma paused to reflect on these words, recognizing that success and courage were essential elements of her journey.

She realized that success was not limited to grand achievements; it could be found in everyday victories, no matter how small. It was the determination to overcome obstacles, the commitment to personal growth, and the willingness to embrace challenges with open arms.

Courage, on the other hand, was the driving force behind success. Emma understood that courage was not the absence of fear but the strength to act despite it. It was the willingness to take risks, to face adversity, and to persevere in the face of doubt.

As the days passed, Emma found herself setting new goals and pursuing dreams she had once considered out of reach. She took on challenges with a newfound sense of courage, drawing inspiration from the daily quotes that reminded her of her own strength.

Emma's journey was not without its share of setbacks and obstacles, but she faced them with unwavering determination. She understood that every stumble was a chance to learn and grow, and every challenge was an opportunity to demonstrate her courage.

As the chapter continued, Emma's success was not defined solely by external achievements but by her personal growth and resilience. She had become a testament to the power of positivity, success, and courage, and her journey was inspiring others to embark on their own paths of self-discovery and transformation.

With each new day, Emma felt her courage growing, and her sense of success deepening. She was living proof that positivity could ignite the flames of success and courage, illuminating the path toward a life well-lived.

As she closed the book for the day, Emma felt a sense of pride and accomplishment. The journey had brought her closer to her dreams, and she knew that there was much more to uncover in the chapters that lay ahead. Success and courage had become her companions on this remarkable voyage of self-discovery, and she was ready to embrace whatever challenges and triumphs awaited her.

Chapter 5: Finding Your Joy

With each chapter of her year-long journey through positivity, Emma discovered new facets of her inner self. As she turned the page to Chapter 5, titled "Finding Your Joy," she couldn't help but feel a sense of anticipation. The daily quotes had already sparked a transformation in her, and she was eager to explore the role of joy in her life.

The first quote in this chapter read, **"Joy is the secret ingredient that infuses life with meaning. It can be found in the simplest of moments and the smallest of pleasures. Embrace it, and watch your days become brighter."** Emma paused to reflect on these words, realizing that joy was a vital part of her journey.

She had always been a practical person, focused on her goals and responsibilities. But this chapter encouraged her to seek joy in the ordinary, to find happiness in everyday moments, and to savor the simple pleasures of life.

As the days passed, Emma began to notice the beauty in the small things. She marveled at the colors of a sunset, savored the taste of her morning coffee, and found joy in the laughter of friends. She discovered that joy was not a distant destination; it was a state of mind that could be cultivated every day.

Emma also realized that joy was contagious. When she shared her moments of happiness with others, it had a ripple effect, spreading positivity and laughter. She found herself becoming a source of joy for her friends and family, and her relationships grew stronger as a result.

The chapter not only encouraged Emma to find her joy but also inspired her to create moments of joy for others. She embarked on acts of kindness and shared her positivity with those in need. Emma's journey was not just about self-discovery; it was about spreading the joy she had found to the world.

As the chapter continued, Emma's life became a tapestry of moments, each woven with threads of joy. She was no longer bound by the limitations of practicality; she had embraced the magic of joy and allowed it to guide her steps.

With each new day, Emma's joy grew stronger, and her life became more vibrant. She understood that positivity was not just about facing challenges with a smile; it was about finding the light in every moment and allowing it to shine brightly.

As she closed the book for the day, Emma felt a

deep sense of contentment. The journey had taken her to new heights of happiness, and she was eager to discover what the remaining chapters held. Joy had become her constant companion, and she knew that it would guide her through the twists and turns of the path ahead.

Chapter 6: The Path to Positivity and Success

Emma's year-long journey through positivity had been a profound transformation, and the next chapter, "The Path to Positivity and Success," promised to take her to new heights. As she opened the book, she felt a surge of excitement, knowing that the daily quotes had already become an integral part of her life.

The first quote in this chapter read, **"Success is not the destination but the journey itself. It is the daily reminders and small steps that lead to significant personal growth. Embrace the path, and you will reach the summit."** Emma pondered these words, recognizing the significance of her ongoing journey.

This chapter emphasized the idea that success was not limited to grand achievements but was the result of consistent effort and perseverance.

Emma realized that every day was an opportunity for growth, a chance to take small steps toward her goals.

With each passing day, she found herself setting new goals and seeking opportunities for personal development. The daily quotes provided her with guidance, encouraging her to stay focused and determined. Emma knew that success was not an overnight accomplishment; it was the sum of her daily efforts.

The chapter also emphasized the importance of resilience and determination in the face of challenges. Emma understood that obstacles were a natural part of any journey, and her ability to overcome them was a testament to her growth and strength.

As she moved through the chapter, Emma found herself becoming more resilient, more determined, and more committed to her goals. The journey was not without its share of setbacks, but she faced them with unwavering determination, drawing inspiration from the daily quotes.

Emma's success was no longer defined solely by external achievements but by her personal growth and resilience. She realized that her journey was not about reaching a specific destination but about the path itself, the daily reminders of positivity, and the small steps that led to significant change.

With each new day, Emma's path became clearer, and her sense of purpose deepened. She understood that success was not an end goal but a continuous journey, a way of life that led to positivity, personal growth, and fulfillment.

As she closed the book for the day, Emma felt a sense of empowerment. The journey had already taken her far, and she knew that there was much more to discover in the chapters that lay ahead. The path to positivity and success had become her daily companion, guiding her steps and reminding her that every day was an opportunity for growth.

Chapter 7: A Year of Love, Hope, and Happiness

With the turning of the pages, Emma's journey through positivity took on a new dimension as she entered Chapter 7, titled "A Year of Love, Hope, and Happiness." The daily quotes had already infused her life with renewed purpose, but this chapter promised to explore the depth of these emotions in her journey.

The first quote in this chapter read, **"Love, hope, and happiness are the cornerstones of a life well-lived. They are the threads that weave the tapestry of our existence. Embrace them, and your life will be filled with warmth and light."** Emma reflected on these words, recognizing the profound significance of these emotions.

Love, she thought, was the force that bound people together, the source of connection and compassion. It was the love of family and friends that had sustained her through difficult times, and she had found herself cherishing those relationships more than ever.

Hope was the spark that ignited her dreams and aspirations. It was the belief that tomorrow could be better than today, and Emma understood that hope was the driving force behind her journey. It fueled her determination and kept her focused on her goals.

Happiness, the third cornerstone, was the joy that colored her daily life. Emma realized that happiness could be found in the simplest of moments, and she had begun to savor every experience, no matter how small. Her heart was filled with gratitude for the moments that brought joy and laughter.

As the days turned into weeks, Emma's life became a tapestry woven with threads of love, hope, and happiness. She had learned to embrace these emotions fully and to share them with others. Her friends and family saw her as a source of warmth and light, and her relationships grew stronger as a result.

The chapter encouraged Emma not only to find these emotions in her life but also to inspire them in others. She embarked on acts of kindness and shared her positivity, love, hope, and happiness with those in need. Her journey was not just about self-discovery; it was about spreading these emotions to the world.

With each new day, Emma's love grew stronger, her hope brighter, and her happiness deeper. She knew that positivity was not just about a personal journey; it was about creating a world where love, hope, and happiness were abundant and accessible to all.

As she closed the book for the day, Emma felt a deep sense of contentment. The journey had taken her to new heights of love, hope, and happiness, and she was eager to discover what the remaining chapters held. These emotions had become her constant companions, guiding her through the path ahead and reminding her of the warmth and light they could bring to her life and the lives of others.

Chapter 8: Unleash Your Potential

As Emma's journey through the year of positivity continued, she found herself eagerly opening the book to Chapter 8, titled "Unleash Your Potential." The daily quotes had already kindled a transformation within her, and she was ready to explore the untapped capabilities and dreams that lay within.

The first quote in this chapter read, **"Your potential is like a hidden treasure waiting to be discovered. It's the key to unlocking your dreams and turning them into reality. Embrace it, and watch how your life transforms."** Emma pondered these words, realizing that her potential was a vital part of her ongoing journey.

The chapter emphasized that one's potential was not limited by past accomplishments or current circumstances. It was the latent abilities, talents, and dreams that often remained unexplored. Emma understood that her journey was about uncovering her potential and transforming it into meaningful actions.

As the days passed, Emma found herself setting new goals and pursuing dreams she had once considered out of reach. She understood that her potential was not confined to her comfort zone; it lay beyond it. The daily quotes provided guidance, motivating her to push boundaries and dare to dream bigger.

The chapter also emphasized the importance of perseverance and determination in the journey of realizing one's potential. Emma recognized that the path to self-discovery and growth was not without challenges, but she faced them with unwavering determination. Each obstacle became an opportunity to prove her potential.

Emma's journey was not solely about achieving external success; it was about reaching the depths of her inner self and uncovering the potential that had always resided within her. With each new day, she discovered new capabilities and honed her skills, allowing her potential to shine brightly.

As the chapter continued, Emma realized that she was not alone in this journey. She was part of a community of like-minded individuals who sought to discover and unleash their own potential. She found inspiration in their stories and shared her experiences, becoming a source of motivation for others.

With each new day, Emma's potential grew stronger, and her life became a canvas on which she could paint her dreams. She understood that positivity was not just about facing challenges with a smile; it was about discovering and nurturing the potential within, and allowing it to guide her steps.

As she closed the book for the day, Emma felt a profound sense of purpose. The journey had already taken her to new heights of self-discovery and growth, and she knew that there was much more to uncover in the chapters that lay ahead. Unleashing her potential had become a daily commitment, and she was ready to embrace whatever challenges and triumphs awaited her.

Chapter 9: A Brighter Tomorrow

As Emma's journey through the year of positivity continued, she felt a sense of anticipation when she turned the page to Chapter 9, titled "A Brighter Tomorrow." The daily quotes had already ignited a transformation within her, and she was eager to explore the role of positivity in creating a better future.

The first quote in this chapter read, **"Positivity is the compass that guides you to a brighter tomorrow. It inspires hope and motivates change. Embrace it, and watch how your future unfolds."** Emma pondered these words, recognizing the profound significance of positivity in shaping her destiny.

This chapter emphasized that positivity was not just about the present moment; it was a powerful force that could inspire hope and motivate change. Emma realized that her journey was about cultivating a positive mindset and using it as a driving force to create a better future.

As the days passed, Emma found herself envisioning a brighter tomorrow. She set new goals, both for herself and for her community, and she took action to make those goals a reality. The daily quotes provided guidance, reminding her that every step toward a brighter future began with a positive mindset.

The chapter also emphasized the importance of hope and resilience in the face of challenges. Emma understood that obstacles were a natural part of any journey, but her unwavering determination allowed her to overcome them. She believed that a brighter tomorrow was not just a dream but an achievable reality.

Emma's journey was not solely about personal growth; it was about making a positive impact on the world around her. She realized that by sharing her positivity and inspiring hope, she could contribute to a better future for her community and beyond.

With each new day, Emma's vision of a brighter tomorrow grew clearer, and her determination to make it a reality deepened. She understood that positivity was not just a personal choice but a collective one, and it was a force that could drive positive change in the world.

As the chapter continued, Emma felt a renewed sense of purpose. She knew that her journey had the power to inspire hope and motivate change, not just for herself but for those around her. Positivity had become the compass guiding her toward a brighter tomorrow, and she was ready to embrace the opportunities and challenges that lay ahead.

As she closed the book for the day, Emma felt a profound sense of optimism. The journey had already taken her far, and she knew that there was much more to discover in the chapters that lay ahead. A brighter tomorrow had become her daily motivation, and she was determined to continue her positive impact on the world.

Chapter 10: A Life Well-Lived

With each turning of the page, Emma's year-long journey through positivity took on a deeper significance as she reached Chapter 10, titled "A Life Well-Lived." The daily quotes had already instilled in her a newfound sense of purpose, but this chapter promised to explore the ultimate goal of her journey: living a life filled with positivity and fulfillment.

The first quote in this chapter read, **"A life well-lived is a testament to the power of positivity. It is a life rich in love, hope, happiness, and success. Embrace it, and you will leave a lasting legacy of inspiration."** Emma reflected on these words, realizing that the culmination of her journey was a life that had embraced the core values of positivity.

This chapter emphasized that a life well-lived was not just about personal success; it was about creating a meaningful legacy that inspired others. Emma understood that her journey was about leaving a positive impact on the world and encouraging others to embark on their paths of self-discovery and transformation.

As the days passed, Emma found herself focused on the larger picture, not just her personal growth but the positive impact she could have on her community and the world. She set out to make a difference, to inspire others to embrace love, hope, happiness, and success.

The chapter also emphasized the importance of reflection and gratitude. Emma realized that to live a life well-lived, she needed to appreciate the journey and acknowledge the positive changes it had brought to her. Gratitude was the key to finding contentment and fulfillment.

With each new day, Emma's determination to live a life well-lived grew stronger, and she understood that her journey was not just about achieving her goals but about sharing her experiences and inspiring others.

As the chapter continued, Emma saw her life as a canvas on which she could paint a legacy of positivity. She knew that her journey was not just a personal quest but a testament to the power of positivity and the potential for transformation that lay within each individual.

With each new day, Emma was reminded that positivity was not just a mindset; it was a way of life, a way to create a life well-lived. She was ready to embrace the challenges and triumphs that lay ahead, knowing that her journey was a testament to the transformative power of positivity.

As she closed the book for the day, Emma felt a profound sense of purpose. The journey had taken her to new heights of positivity, and she knew that her life was becoming a testament to the power of love, hope, happiness, and success. Emma was ready to carry the torch of positivity forward, inspiring others to embrace the journey of self-discovery and transformation.

Conclusion: Carrying Positivity Forward

As Emma reached the final pages of her year-long journey through positivity, she felt a sense of completion and a profound sense of gratitude. The journey had taken her on a transformative path, igniting her spirit and inspiring her to embrace a life filled with love, hope, happiness, and success.

The conclusion of the book emphasized that carrying positivity forward was not just a choice but a responsibility. Emma understood that her journey was not meant to be a solitary one; it was a testament to the power of positivity and the potential for transformation that lay within every individual.

She recognized that her journey was just the beginning of a lifelong commitment to embracing positivity and inspiring others to do the same. Emma knew that she had the power to create a ripple effect of positivity, touching the lives of her friends, family, and community.

The conclusion of the book reiterates the significance of living a life well-lived, one that is rich in love, hope, happiness, and success. It encouraged Emma to continue inspiring hope and motivating change, not just for herself but for those around her.

With each new day, Emma was reminded that positivity was not just a mindset; it was a way of life. She was ready to carry the torch of positivity forward, and as she closed the book, she felt a deep sense of purpose and fulfillment.

The journey had left an indelible mark on her, and she knew that her life was becoming a testament to the transformative power of positivity. As she stepped into a future filled with love, hope, happiness, and success, Emma was eager to inspire others to embark on their own paths of self-discovery and transformation, leaving a lasting legacy of inspiration for generations to come.

25 Quotes to Illuminate Your Day with Radiance

In the grand tapestry of life, we find the threads of wisdom interwoven, each quote akin to a brilliant star that guides us through the vast expanse of existence. Let us embark on a journey through these 25 quotes, which are not mere words but the shimmering gems of inspiration. They brighten your day, much like the sun's rays painting the morning sky.

1. "Life is a boundless canvas, and with every dawn, we become artists, brushing our stories in vibrant strokes of destiny."
2. "In the garden of existence, each day unfurls as a new bloom, inviting us to embrace the untamed beauty of life."
3. "Life's brilliance lies in its unpredictability, like an ever-shifting mosaic of experiences that dance in the kaleidoscope of our days."
4. "The dance of life orchestrates a mesmerizing waltz, with its ebb and flow, where emotions twirl and hearts find their rhythm."
5. "Our life's journey is an epic tale, chapters filled with trials and triumphs, each one a precious gem that adorns the necklace of our memories."
6. "The sunflower teaches us resilience, for it turns its face towards the sun, even on the darkest of days, reminding us to seek light amidst the shadows."
7. "The voyage of life is a captivating journey, akin to sailing uncharted waters, with each ripple concealing

the promise of discovery."

8. "In the cosmic ballet of existence, every day is a celestial performance, and we are the spectators and dancers of this marvelous show."

9. "Life's labyrinth may confound, but within its winding paths, we uncover the treasures of resilience and the map to our dreams."

10. "In the symphony of existence, every sunrise is a harmonious note, composing melodies of hope and inviting us to sing along."

11. "The tapestry of our existence is woven with threads of joy and sorrow, and it's in the contrast that we find the beauty of life."

12. "Like the ever-turning pages of a book, life's chapters unfold, revealing the unpredictable plotlines that shape our destinies."

13. "Each day is a blank canvas, and with the brushstrokes of our choices, we paint the masterpiece of our lives, a work in progress."

14. "The river of time flows ceaselessly, and in its waters, we find the reflection of our past, the beauty of the present, and the promises of the future."

15. "Life is the grand tapestry where our choices are threads, weaving stories of love, adventure, and resilience into the fabric of existence."

16. "Amidst life's intricate patterns, we discover that each obstacle is a stepping stone, leading us toward the pinnacle of our dreams."

17. "Every sunrise whispers the promise of a new beginning, a chance to seize the day and paint the canvas of existence with radiant hues."

18. "In the symphony of existence, each day composes a

new movement, and we are the conductors of our destinies, orchestrating our own melodies."

19. "Life is a treasure chest of memories, and with each passing day, we unearth precious gems that illuminate our journey."

20. "The journey of life is an intricate maze, and every twist and turn is an opportunity to find inspiration, resilience, and unexpected beauty."

21. "Within the labyrinth of existence, we find that every obstacle is a challenge to conquer, a chance to illuminate our path with the torch of determination."

22. "Life's story is written with the ink of experiences, and every chapter, whether joyous or challenging, contributes to the epic tale."

23. "Each day is a chapter in the book of our lives, waiting to be written with the ink of choices, the prose of dreams, and the poetry of emotions."

24. "In the grand narrative of existence, every day is a page in the book of life, an opportunity to pen our own stories of inspiration."

25. "Life's journey is a masterful novel, filled with unpredictable twists and turns, yet its pages are illuminated by the wisdom we gain along the way."

25 Heartwarming Love Quotes to Ignite the Soul

In the grand tapestry of human emotions, love is the vibrant thread that weaves together the stories of our hearts. These 25 love quotes are not mere words; they are the whispers of the heart, the flames of passion, and the solace of companionship. Let them envelop your soul in a warm embrace, much like a cozy blanket on a winter's day.

1. "Love, a rare gem, is forged in the fires of connection, destined to shine eternally in the treasure chest of our hearts."
2. "In the symphony of the heart, love's melody is the sweetest, an ode to our shared humanity that resonates in every beat."
3. "True love is the celestial bridge that unites two souls in the dance of eternity, a connection that defies time and space."
4. "Love, the universal language, is whispered by the stars and echoed by the heart, a cosmic conversation that knows no boundaries."
5. "Love, an intoxicating elixir, turns ordinary moments into extraordinary memories, infusing the mundane with magic."
6. "In the garden of love, every glance is a blossoming flower, every touch a gentle caress, and every word a sonnet of affection."
7. "The moon and the sun share a celestial dance, just as love and passion waltz together in the theater of the

heart, an eternal performance."

8. "True love is like a fine wine, growing richer with time, its flavors deepening into a symphony of shared experiences."

9. "Love is a kaleidoscope of emotions, each facet revealing a different shade of affection, from the tender to the passionate."

10. "In the embrace of love, every day is a new chapter, an opportunity to write a story of companionship and devotion."

11. "Love, like a gentle breeze, soothes the soul, reminding us that even the most turbulent days can find tranquility."

12. "Two hearts in harmony create a symphony of love, their melodies resonating with the echoes of their shared dreams."

13. "The tapestry of love is woven with threads of laughter, tears, and tender moments, each forming a unique and intricate pattern."

14. "Love's journey is a celestial voyage, where two souls navigate the cosmic sea of existence, guided by the stars of their affection."

15. "In the grand mosaic of life, love is the masterpiece, each piece carefully placed, forming a picture of joy and unity."

16. "Love is the sanctuary where we find solace from life's storms, a refuge where the heart can weather any tempest."

17. "Every love story is a sonnet, written in the language of the heart, with verses of passion and stanzas of devotion."

18. "Love's embrace is a gentle sanctuary, where we find not

only warmth but the courage to face life's challenges."

19. "In the symphony of love, every kiss is a note, and every touch is a chord, composing melodies of affection that serenade the heart."

20. "Love, a treasure hidden in the vault of the soul, becomes more valuable with every shared moment and memory."

21. "The path of love is illuminated by the stars of shared dreams, guiding two hearts toward a future filled with endless possibilities."

22. "Love, like a lighthouse, shines its radiant beam on the shores of our souls, guiding us through the darkest nights."

23. "Every moment in love is a verse, a stanza, a chapter, an ongoing narrative that tells the story of two hearts intertwined."

24. "In the garden of affection, every glance is a blossoming flower, every touch a gentle caress, and every word a sonnet of love."

25. "Love's story is not told in words alone but in the tender gazes, the shared laughter, and the gentle touches that speak the language of the heart."

25 Inspirational Quotes for Unwavering Motivation

1. "Success is a journey, not a destination. Keep striving, keep thriving, and embrace the adventure."
2. "The path to success is not always a straight line. Embrace the twists and turns, for they shape your unique journey."
3. "Success is a reflection of determination. The harder you work, the brighter your success shines."
4. "In the pursuit of success, enthusiasm is your compass, and diligence is your vehicle."
5. "The seeds of success are sown in persistence. Water them with dedication, and watch them flourish."
6. "Success is the sweetest victory, a testament to the strength of your spirit and the power of your dreams."
7. "Achievement is the melody of ambition. Keep playing the tune of your goals with unwavering dedication."
8. "In the realm of success, obstacles are stepping stones to greatness. Use them as your path to triumph."
9. "Success is the art of turning your aspirations into actions, one brushstroke at a time."
10. "The road to success is paved with hard work and determination, and every step takes you closer to your dreams."
11. "Your journey to success may have setbacks, but each one is a setup for a comeback."
12. "Success is the story of dedication, where every chapter tells of your commitment to your goals."
13. "The key to success is consistency. Keep showing up,

keep pushing forward, and keep reaching higher."

14. "Success is the sum of small efforts repeated day in and day out. Every action matters."

15. "In the tapestry of success, each challenge adds a vibrant thread, making the final masterpiece more exquisite."

16. "Success is the sweetest fruit of perseverance, a reminder that dreams achieved are the most satisfying."

17. "To taste success, you must first savor the journey. Every moment is a step forward."

18. "In the grand story of success, you are the author, and every decision is a stroke of the pen."

19. "Success is the result of unwavering dedication and the courage to keep going when the path is challenging."

20. "To reach the stars of success, you must first set your goals high and reach for them with determination."

21. "Success is like a grand puzzle. Every effort is a piece, and when you fit them together, you reveal a beautiful picture."

22. "In the symphony of success, your actions are the notes that compose a beautiful melody of achievement."

23. "Success is the destination, but the journey is where you find the treasures of experience and wisdom."

24. "To achieve success, you must first believe in yourself. Your self-confidence is the foundation of your dreams."

25. "In the world of success, every step you take is a stroke on the canvas of your achievements, painting a masterpiece of your life."

25 Uplifting Quotes to Elevate Your Spirit

1. "Happiness is not a destination; it's a beautiful journey. Embrace every moment and savor its sweet nectar."
2. "In the garden of the soul, happiness blooms like a vibrant flower, inviting us to embrace its scent."
3. "True happiness is a treasure hidden in the simplest moments, waiting to be discovered in the everyday."
4. "Happiness is not found in the pursuit of perfection but in the acceptance of imperfections."
5. "Like a butterfly, happiness flutters into our lives when we least expect it, bringing joy on delicate wings."
6. "In the symphony of life, happiness is the sweetest melody, a tune that resonates in the heart of the joyful."
7. "Happiness is the key that unlocks the door to a world filled with smiles, laughter, and the warmth of contentment."
8. "The pursuit of happiness is an art, with every moment a brushstroke on the canvas of contentment."
9. "True happiness is found not in abundance but in the appreciation of life's simple pleasures."
10. "In the grand mosaic of existence, every moment of happiness is a shimmering tile, creating a brilliant masterpiece."
11. "The laughter of today becomes the cherished memories of tomorrow, a gift that keeps on giving."
12. "Happiness is not a destination to reach but a state of being to embrace."
13. "In the theater of life, happiness takes center stage, ready to perform its most heartwarming acts."
14. "The treasure of happiness is found within; it's the light

that guides you through life's darkest tunnels."

15. "Happiness is the elixir of the heart, infusing every moment with the sweetness of joy."

16. "In the garden of life, happiness is the vibrant blossom that brightens the dullest of days."

17. "Happiness is the sunshine that breaks through the clouds of life's challenges, reminding us that brighter days await."

18. "The pursuit of happiness is not a race; it's a leisurely stroll through life, savoring the beauty of each step."

19. "Happiness is the gentle whisper that dances on the breeze, a reminder to appreciate life's simple pleasures."

20. "In the grand story of existence, happiness is the recurring motif that brings harmony to the soul."

21. "The heart's capacity for happiness is boundless, and it expands with every moment of gratitude."

22. "Happiness is the secret to a life well-lived, an ever-present companion in the journey of existence."

23. "In the symphony of joy, every note of happiness creates a masterpiece of harmonious living."

24. "Happiness is the compass that guides us through life's labyrinth, showing the way to a contented heart."

25. "In the world of emotions, happiness is the North Star, a constant presence that illuminates our path to fulfillment."

25 Inspirational Quotes to Ignite Courage

1. "Courage is the fire that burns within the heart, a beacon of hope that shines in the darkest hours."
2. "In the theater of life, courage takes center stage, ready to perform heroic acts that inspire and uplift."
3. "Every daring step forward is a testament to the valor of the human spirit, a reminder that we can overcome any challenge."
4. "Courage is the bridge that carries us over turbulent waters, leading to a world filled with endless possibilities."
5. "Bravery is a symphony of resilience, composed by those who refuse to yield to adversity."
6. "In the garden of the soul, courage is the vibrant bud that blossoms into the resplendent flower of determination."
7. "Courage is the elixir of fear, transforming it into the fuel for audacious actions and inspiring feats."
8. "Like a lighthouse in a storm, courage guides us through life's most tumultuous waters, showing us the way to safety."
9. "Courage is not the absence of fear but the strength to move forward despite it, conquering the shadows of doubt."
10. "In the grand narrative of existence, courage is the thread that weaves together tales of triumph over adversity."
11. "The path of courage is not devoid of obstacles; it's a trailblazing journey marked by unwavering

determination."

12. "Courage is the heart's secret weapon, the catalyst for conquering the most formidable challenges."

13. "In the symphony of bravery, every act of courage is a note that adds to the harmonious melody of determination."

14. "Courage is the armor that protects us in life's battles, empowering us to face adversity with unwavering strength."

15. "In the tapestry of courage, each obstacle faced becomes a vibrant thread, creating a resilient and magnificent pattern."

16. "Courage is the anthem of the indomitable spirit, sung by those who defy the odds and rise above life's trials."

17. "The path of courage may be challenging, but every step is a testament to the power of the human will."

18. "Courage is the strength to continue even when it seems impossible, a force that pushes us beyond our limits."

19. "In the cosmic voyage of life, courage is the North Star, guiding us through the infinite universe of possibilities."

20. "Courage is the master key to unlocking the doors of opportunity, for it opens the way to uncharted territory."

21. "The garden of courage is where the seeds of determination are sown, and the blossoms of resilience bloom."

22. "Courage is the symphony of bravery, with every act contributing to a magnificent and awe-inspiring composition."

23. "In the grand epic of life, courage is the hero's journey, filled with challenges and triumphs that inspire."

24. "Courage is the unshakable belief in one's ability to rise

above adversity, to conquer the highest peaks of achievement."

25. "In the world of emotions, courage is the guiding star, illuminating our path to self-discovery and the limitless potential of the human spirit."

25 Inspirational Quotes to Illuminate Your Path with Hope

1. "Hope is the gentle light that guides us through the labyrinth of despair, showing the way to brighter horizons."
2. "In the realm of hope, even the smallest spark can ignite a wildfire of positive change, illuminating the darkest nights."
3. "Hope is the heartbeat of resilience, a constant reminder that tomorrow can be better than today, that every dawn brings new possibilities."
4. "As the phoenix rises from its ashes, hope emerges from the darkest nights, bearing the promise of a new day."
5. "In the garden of life, hope is the fragile bud that blossoms into a resplendent flower of possibility, reminding us that growth is inevitable."
6. "Hope is the muse of dreams, whispering inspiration into the ears of the imaginative and encouraging them to reach for the stars."
7. "In the symphony of hope, every note is a promise, and every melody is a testament to the strength of the human spirit."
8. "Hope is the compass that points to the brighter side of life, reminding us that even in the most challenging times, there's a glimmer of possibility."
9. "The tapestry of hope is woven with threads of resilience and the unbreakable spirit of those who refuse to give up."

10. "Hope is the eternal flame that burns in our hearts, lighting the way through the darkest nights and leading us to a brighter tomorrow."

11. "In the grand story of existence, hope is the recurring theme that encourages us to keep turning the pages of our lives."

12. "Hope is not the absence of despair but the belief that even in the depths of darkness, there is a path towards the light."

13. "The path of hope may be challenging, but every step is a reminder that the journey is worth every obstacle."

14. "Hope is the North Star that guides us through life's turbulent seas, offering us solace and a sense of direction."

15. "In the cosmic dance of emotions, hope is the radiant star that lights up the night sky, offering guidance and inspiration."

16. "Hope is the anthem of perseverance, sung by those who refuse to surrender to life's trials and tribulations."

17. "The journey of hope may have setbacks, but each one is a setup for a comeback, a reminder that resilience prevails."

18. "Hope is the strength that pulls us forward, the force that urges us to reach for a brighter tomorrow."

19. "In the garden of the soul, hope is the eternal spring, a constant source of renewal and inspiration."

20. "Hope is the symphony of belief, with every note adding to the harmonious melody of determination and possibility."

21. "The garden of hope is where the seeds of determination are sown, and the blossoms of resilience bloom."

22. "Hope is the guiding star that illuminates the path to our dreams, leading us through the boundless universe of possibilities."
23. "In the grand epic of life, hope is the hero's journey, filled with challenges and triumphs that inspire us to reach for the stars."
24. "Hope is the unshakable belief in one's ability to rise above adversity, to conquer the highest peaks of achievement."
25. "In the world of emotions, hope is the guiding star, illuminating our path to self-discovery and the limitless potential of the human spirit."

100 Quotes for a Richer, Healthier, and Happier You

1. "Laugh at yourself first before anyone else can." - Elsa Maxwell
2. "A day without sunshine is like, you know, night." - Steve

Martin
3. "I'm writing a book. I've got the page numbers done." - Steven Wright
4. "Happiness is having a large, loving, caring, close-knit family in another city." - George Burns
5. "I intend to live forever, or die trying." - Groucho Marx
6. "I'm on the whiskey diet. I've lost three days already." - Tommy Cooper
7. "The best way to teach your kids about taxes is by eating 30% of their ice cream." - Bill Murray
8. "I've developed a new philosophy... I only dread one day at a time." - Charlie Brown (Charles M. Schulz)
9. "When I was a kid, my parents moved a lot, but I always found them." - Rodney Dangerfield
10. "If you think you are too small to make a difference, try sleeping with a mosquito." - Dalai Lama
11. "My grandmother started walking five miles a day when she was sixty. She's ninety-seven now, and we don't know where the heck she is." - Ellen DeGeneres
12. "I couldn't repair your brakes, so I made your horn louder." - Steven Wright
13. "I don't want to achieve immortality through my work; I want to achieve immortality through not dying." - Woody Allen
14. "I used to sell furniture for a living. The trouble was, it was my own." - Les Dawson
15. "Do not take life too seriously. You will never get out of it alive." - Elbert Hubbard
16. "Behind every great man, there is a woman rolling her eyes." - Jim Carrey
17. "A bank is a place that will lend you money if you can prove that you don't need it." - Bob Hope

18. "I am free of all prejudice. I hate everyone equally." - W.C. Fields
19. "The road to success is dotted with many tempting parking spaces." - Will Rogers
20. "I'm writing a book. I've got the page numbers done." - Steven Wright
21. "You can't have everything. Where would you put it?" - Steven Wright
22. "Life is what happens when you're busy making other plans." - John Lennon
23. "I'm not arguing, I'm just explaining why I'm right." - Unknown
24. "I'm writing a book. I've got the page numbers done." - Steven Wright
25. "When I'm sad, I stop being sad and be awesome instead." - Barney Stinson
26. "You're only given a little spark of madness. You mustn't lose it." - Robin Williams
27. "If at first you don't succeed, then skydiving definitely isn't for you." - Steven Wright
28. "The only mystery in life is why the kamikaze pilots wore helmets." - Al McGuire
29. "I never feel more alone than when I'm trying to put sunscreen on my back." - Jimmy Kimmel
30. "I used to be a people person, but people ruined that for me." - Unknown
31. "I have a simple philosophy: Fill what's empty. Empty what's full. Scratch where it itches." - Alice Roosevelt Longworth
32. "I'm in shape. Round is a shape." - George Carlin
33. "Honest criticism is hard to take, particularly from a relative, a friend, an acquaintance, or a stranger." -

Franklin P. Jones

34. "I have not failed. I've just found 10,000 ways that won't work." - Thomas A. Edison

35. "Age is merely the number of years the world has been enjoying you. Congratulations on your birthday!" - Unknown

36. "I find television very educational. Every time someone turns it on, I go into another room and read a book." - Groucho Marx

37. "The worst time to have a heart attack is during a game of charades." - Demetri Martin

38. "Marriage is the main reason for divorce." - Unknown

39. "Why do they call it rush hour when nothing moves?" - Robin Williams

40. "The early bird might get the worm, but the second mouse gets the cheese." - Steven Wright

41. "It's not the size of the dog in the fight, it's the size of the fight in the dog." - Mark Twain

42. "When I was a boy, I laid in my twin-sized bed and wondered where my brother was." - Mitch Hedberg

43. "I'm writing a book. I've got the page numbers done." - Steven Wright

44. "The only thing that ever sat its way to success was a hen." - Sarah Brown

45. "A clear conscience is a sure sign of a bad memory." - Mark Twain

46. "Some people are like clouds. When they disappear, it's a brighter day." - Unknown

47. "You can't make everybody happy. You're not a jar of Nutella." - Unknown

48. "Do not argue with an idiot. He will drag you down to his level and beat you with experience." - Unknown

49. "The trouble with having an open mind, of course, is that people will insist on coming along and trying to put things in it." - Terry Pratchett
50. "To succeed in life, you need two things: ignorance and confidence." - Mark Twain
51. "The only time to be positive you've got a clear path is when you're on the edge of a cliff." - Anonymous
52. "When tempted to fight fire with fire, remember that the Fire Department usually uses water." - Unknown
53. "To steal ideas from one person is plagiarism; to steal from many is research." - Steven Wright
54. "If you steal from one author, it's plagiarism; if you steal from many, it's research." - Wilson Mizner
55. "Behind every great man, there is a woman rolling her eyes." - Jim Carrey
56. "I don't need a hair stylist, my pillow gives me a new hairstyle every morning." - Unknown
57. "I'm writing a book. I've got the page numbers done." - Steven Wright
58. "I refuse to answer that question on the grounds that I don't know the answer." - Douglas Adams
59. "If you're too open-minded, your brains will fall out." - Lawrence Ferlinghetti
60. "Life is like a sewer... what you get out of it depends on what you put into it." - Tom Lehrer
61. "Always forgive your enemies; nothing annoys them so much." - Oscar Wilde
62. "Never put off until tomorrow what you can do the day after tomorrow." - Mark Twain
63. "The road to success is dotted with many tempting parking spaces." - Will Rogers
64. "To succeed in life, you need two things: ignorance and

confidence." - Mark Twain

65. "I'm writing a book. I've got the page numbers done." - Steven Wright

66. "I told my wife she was drawing her eyebrows too high. She looked surprised." - Unknown

67. "I'm on the whiskey diet. I've lost three days already." - Tommy Cooper

68. "I intend to live forever, or die trying." - Groucho Marx

69. "Happiness is having a large, loving, caring, close-knit family in another city." - George Burns

70. "I used to sell furniture for a living. The trouble was, it was my own." - Les Dawson

71. "A day without sunshine is like, you know, night." - Steve Martin

72. "If you think you are too small to make a difference, try sleeping with a mosquito." - Dalai Lama

73. "My grandmother started walking five miles a day when she was sixty. She's ninety-seven now, and we don't know where the heck she is." - Ellen DeGeneres

74. "I'm not arguing, I'm just explaining why I'm right." - Unknown

75. "I couldn't repair your brakes, so I made your horn louder." - Steven Wright

76. "My financial advisor told me to invest in laughter, and I've been rolling in riches ever since." - Unknown

77. "They say laughter is the best medicine. If that's the case, I must be the picture of health!" - Unknown

78. "I have not failed. I've just found 10,000 ways that won't work." - Thomas A. Edison

79. "They say money can't buy happiness, but it can buy a ticket to a comedy show, and that's pretty close." - Unknown

80. "I've found the key to happiness: It's a good laugh, a hearty meal, and no Wi-Fi for a week!" - Unknown
81. "My doctor prescribed a daily dose of laughter, and now I'm the healthiest hypochondriac in town." - Unknown
82. "I told my scale about my hilarious sense of humor, and it now claims I've lost 50 pounds of stress!" - Unknown
83. "Love, like a rare gem, is forged in the fires of connection, destined to shine eternally." - Unknown
84. "In the symphony of the heart, love's melody is the sweetest, an ode to our shared humanity." - Unknown
85. "True love is the celestial bridge that unites two souls in the dance of eternity." - Unknown
86. "Love is the universal language, whispered by the stars and echoed by the heart." - Unknown
87. "Love, an intoxicating elixir, turns ordinary moments into extraordinary memories." - Unknown
88. "Success is a constellation of dreams, each one shining with the brilliance of ambition." - Unknown
89. "The path to success is marked by determination and paved with the stones of hard work." - Unknown
90. "Success is a journey, not a destination, with milestones to celebrate along the way." - Unknown
91. "Believe in the magic of your aspirations, for success is a symphony of dreams realized." - Unknown
92. "Success is the sweetest victory, a testament to the strength of one's spirit." - Unknown
93. "Happiness is the enchanting melody of life, playing in the hearts of the joyful." - Unknown
94. "The pursuit of happiness is an art, with every moment a brushstroke on the canvas of contentment." - Unknown
95. "True happiness is the treasure hidden in the simplest moments, waiting to be discovered." - Unknown

96. "Happiness is the key that unlocks the door to a world filled with smiles and laughter." - Unknown
97. "In the garden of the soul, happiness blooms like a vibrant flower, inviting us to embrace its scent." - Unknown
98. "Courage is the fire that burns within the heart, a beacon of hope in the darkest hours." - Unknown
99. "In the theater of life, courage takes center stage, ready to perform its heroic acts." - Unknown
100. "Every daring step forward is a testament to the valor of the human spirit." - Unknown

Made in the USA
Monee, IL
26 December 2023